DAYS THAT SHOOK THE WORLD
NOVEMBER 22, 1963

THE KENNEDY ASSASSINATION

DAYS THAT SHOOK THE WORLD

THE KENNEDY ASSASSINATION

NOVEMBER 22, 1963

Liz Gogerly

RAINTREE
STECK-VAUGHN
PUBLISHERS

A Harcourt Company

Austin   New York

www.raintreesteckvaughn.com

DAYS THAT SHOOK THE WORLD

Assassination in Sarajevo Hiroshima
The Chernobyl Disaster The Kennedy Assassination
D-Day The Moon Landing
The Dream of Martin Luther King Pearl Harbor
The Fall of the Berlin Wall The Wall Street Crash

Published by Raintree Steck-Vaughn Publishers,
an imprint of Steck-Vaughn Company

Library of Congress Cataloging-in-Publication Data
Gogerly, Liz.
The Kennedy Assassination
p. cm.—(Days that shook the world)
Includes bibliographical references and index.
Summary: Provides and overview of John Kennedy's presidency, describes the events surrounding his assassination, a nd discusses its impact on the American people and American society.

ISBN 0-7398-5235-3

1. Kennedy, John F. (John Fitzgerald), 1917–1963—Assassination—Juvenile literature.
[1. Kennedy, John F. (John Fitzgerald), 1917-1963—Assassination.] I. Title. II. Series.

E842.9 .G57 2002
973.922'092—dc21
[B]   2001048773

Printed in Italy. Bound in the United States.

1 2 3 4 5 6 7 8 9 0 LB 06 05 04 03 02

Picture Acknowledgments:

Cover and title page pictures: President Kennedy and his wife, Jackie, shortly before the assassination.

We are grateful to the following for permission to reproduce photographs: Camera Press 17, 30 (Robert Jackson/Dallas Times Herald), 37 (Alan Oxley); Corbis, front cover (Bettmann), title page (Bettmann), 6 (Bettmann), 7 (Bettmann), 9 top, 10 (Bettmann), 11 (Bettmann), 12 (Bettmann), 13 bottom (Bettmann), 14 (Dean Conger), 15 (Bettmann), 21 top (Bettmann), 22 (Bettmann), 24 (Bettmann), 25 both (Bettmann), 26, 27 (Wally McNamee), 28, 29 both, 31, 34 (Bettmann), 35 both (Bettmann), 36 (Bettmann), 38 (Flip Schulke), 39 (Bettmann), 40, 41 top (Tim Page), 41 bottom (Bettmann), 42; Photri 19 bottom; Rex Features 8 (Sipa), 9 bottom, 19 top (Sipa), 20 (Sipa), 21 bottom, 23 top, 32 (Farley), 33 (Hulton Deutsch), 46 (Sipa); Topham Picturepoint 13 top, 16 (AP), 18, 43 (AP). Artwork on page 23 by Alex Pang.

CONTENTS

NOVEMBER 22, 1963:
Arrival at Love Field

The president and his wife, Jackie, greet Dallas officials at Love Field airbase. With their movie star looks, the Kennedys always looked good in photos.

FRIDAY, NOVEMBER 22, 1963, is a day that most people over the age of 50 will never forget. Where they were and what they were doing is etched into their memory, because that was the day John F. Kennedy was killed. For all generations the assassination of this youthful and handsome American president remains a mystery. Why did it happen? Who did it? Piecing together the information and looking at the photographs and film of that terrible day cannot answer all the questions, but we can get closer to understanding the events and the personal tragedies—and consider the historical impact.

The day started in an unexceptional way. The Kennedys arrived at Love Field, a military airbase in Dallas, Texas, at 11:37 A.M. Photographs of a tanned, relaxed President Kennedy with his glamorous, smiling wife, Jackie, on this bright Dallas morning are a frightening reminder of how little anyone can know about his or her own future. Jackie clutched a bouquet of red roses. Her now-famous pink Chanel suit and matching pillbox hat were talked about by the waiting press, who seemed as interested in what the sophisticated First Lady was wearing as they were in the president's political reasons for being in Dallas.

There had been speculation about the Kennedys' trip to Texas. The president had even been told it was not a good idea. But the visit was important to raise his profile for the upcoming presidential elections. In the 1960 elections, Kennedy, a Democrat, had won Texas by a small margin. By 1963, however, his popularity there was on a downward spiral, and the state was becoming a Republican stronghold. Conservative groups in the city were hostile toward some of Kennedy's policies, such as his belief in civil rights.

About one month before Kennedy's arrival, there had been an unpleasant incident in Dallas involving the American ambassador to the United Nations (UN), Adlai Stevenson. On a visit to commemorate the anniversary of the UN, Stevenson had been booed and spit on by an angry mob, and struck over the head by a demonstrator. An immediate ban on disruptive behavior at public assemblies was put in place.

With the president's visit imminent, Dallas County was placed on red alert.

On the morning of November 22, 365 police, 45 representatives from the Department of Public Safety, and 15 sheriff's deputies were positioned along the route of the presidential motorcade. Over 2,000 people had turned up at Love Field to give Kennedy a warm reception. Cheers and waving flags greeted the president—everything seemed to be going well.

A Moment in Time

In 1865, almost a century before Kennedy's death, President Abraham Lincoln had also been assassinated. Who could have guessed that the two moments in time would be so strangely connected:

- Both men are shot in the head from behind.
- Lincoln is killed in Ford's Theatre. Kennedy is killed in a car made by Ford.
- Lincoln's secretary, whose name was Kennedy, told Lincoln not to go to the theater. Kennedy's secretary, whose name was Lincoln, told Kennedy not to go to Dallas.
- John Wilkes Booth (Lincoln's assassin) was born in 1839. Lee Harvey Oswald (Kennedy's alleged assassin) was born in 1939.
- Booth shoots Lincoln in a theater before escaping to a barn. Oswald allegedly shoots Kennedy from a warehouse, then flees to a movie theater.

Crowds of well-wishers clambered to shake hands with the Kennedys. Never would an American president walk among his people so freely again.

Joe Kennedy and his sons, John (right) and Joseph, sail to Great Britain in 1938. Joe always believed that Joseph, rather than John, was destined for great things.

JOHN FITZGERALD KENNEDY WAS born in 1917, in Brookline, Massachusetts. He was the great-grandson of Patrick Kennedy, an Irish farm laborer who, in 1848, had emigrated to Boston. John F. Kennedy's father, Joe Kennedy, was a third-generation American dreamer who, in the 1920s, had done well on the Stock Exchange. Joe married Rose Fitzgerald, whose father had been a respected politician and mayor of Boston, and who was also of Irish descent. The merging of Joe's fortune and Rose's ancestral background founded a dynasty that resembled royal families abroad.

Joe and Rose Kennedy had nine children, but Joe never lost sight of the subjects of his major ambitions—money and politics. His clever handling of cash and trust funds meant that his children would each inherit $20 million on their 21st birthdays. During the 1930s, Joe Kennedy was a major supporter of Franklin D.

Roosevelt, and in 1938 was made ambassador to Great Britain. He was fired two years later, when he was so unpopular in wartime Britain that he had become an embarrassment. After his own failure, Joe concentrated his ambitions on his eldest son, Joseph. He instilled in him his own particular philosophy: "Win, win, win—at any cost." But Joseph paid the ultimate price when his fighter plane was shot down in World War II. Joe's attentions then turned to his second son, John.

John F. Kennedy was everything that Joseph had not been—quiet and cautious, yet at the same time forgetful and sloppy. He did, however, become a great scholar. When he graduated from Harvard in 1940, his thesis was published as a book entitled *Why England Slept*. Kennedy would also win a Pulitzer Prize for *Profiles in Courage* (1956), a biography of several heroic senators.

A youthful JFK reveals his ease in front of the camera at the 1952 Democratic National Convention in Chicago.

In September 1953, the Kennedys celebrated their wedding.

John was also sickly. He suffered from many illnesses, including appendicitis, malaria, and jaundice. In 1935 a severe bad back forced him to take a year off from college. He also had chronic allergies and nearly died once from asthma. But John had inherited Joe's "Win, win, win" attitude, and even if he did not have his brother's charms, he still appeared to have everything going for him. John F. Kennedy was wealthy, good-looking, and intelligent. During World War II, when he served as a torpedo boat commander in the South Pacific, he also became a war hero. He was awarded the Purple Heart and the Navy Medal after rescuing his crew from their sinking boat.

In 1946, under his father's guidance, John F. Kennedy—or JFK, as he came to be known—began his political quest. He was elected to Congress as a Democratic Representative from Massachusetts. In 1952 he began a term in the Senate. The following year he married Jacqueline Bouvier.

Jacqueline Bouvier (1929–1994)

John F. Kennedy married into one of New York's most established families. The Bouviers were part of the United States's "high society." From her manicured appearance to her finishing school accent, Jackie Bouvier would give John F. Kennedy the extra polish his political career needed. Although she was just 22 to his 34 when they met, she had traveled in Europe and spoke several languages. She also worked as a photographer for the *Washington Times-Herald*. She had everything the wife of a modern and forward-looking president could require.

"We're going to sell Jack like soap flakes."
—Joe Kennedy, from A Question of Character
by Thomas C. Reeves

T O UNDERSTAND THE IMPACT of John F. Kennedy upon the American public you have to imagine the United States in the late 1950s and early '60s. The economy was in good shape, and new innovations such as television and other mass-produced electrical goods were changing people's lives. Families were expanding and by 1960, the year that Kennedy was nominated by the Democratic party for his presidential campaign, half the American population was under 25 years old. This new generation, known as "baby boomers," had been brought up listening to rock 'n' roll. They had more freedom, money, and choice than any previous generation.

The civil rights movement had begun to stir people's consciences, and there was a growing awareness of social and racial inequality. People were at last questioning the status quo.

Up until 1960 presidents had seemed old, gray, and altogether very traditional. At the age of 42, Kennedy burst onto the scene with a vitality and wit that charmed this younger population. At last, here was somebody with whom they could identify. It was a trump card that Kennedy used again and again to his advantage. During the presidential campaign, he traveled the United States extensively—it was important that as many people as possible see the relaxed and easygoing candidate. Photographs of Kennedy with Jackie and their young daughter, Caroline, were published in magazines and

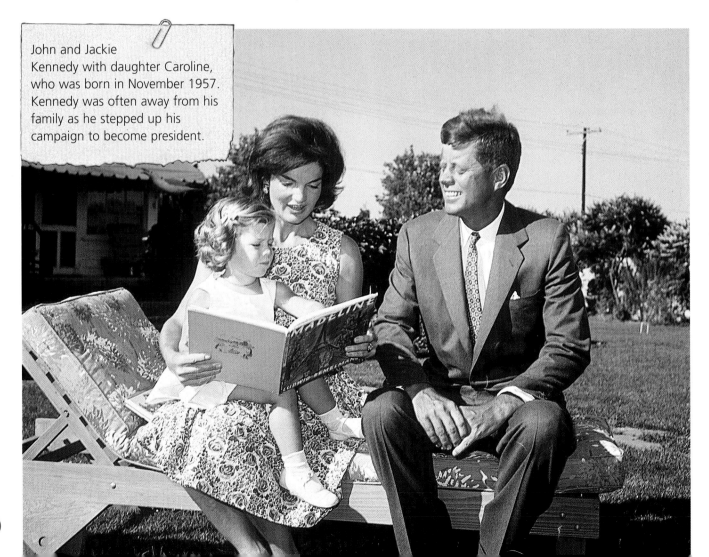

John and Jackie
Kennedy with daughter Caroline, who was born in November 1957. Kennedy was often away from his family as he stepped up his campaign to become president.

In October 1960, Nixon and Kennedy met for a second televised debate. This time Nixon wore makeup to improve his image.

newspapers. In interviews Kennedy was open and self-assured, and he promised change: "The world is changing. The old era is ending. The old ways will not do." This was his message, and it caught on.

It was an election campaign based on image, in the new age of television. In September 1963 the first-ever live, televised debate between Democratic and Republican presidential candidates took place. Before going on the air, Kennedy and his opponent Richard Nixon had been even in the polls, but their screen appearance changed everything. Kennedy was at ease in front of the cameras, and appeared healthy and handsome. Nixon, who had recently been ill, looked clammy and pale, with a five o'clock shadow. Kennedy's confident appearance shifted public opinion in his favor. For the first time, the power of television had become apparent. A student later told Kennedy, "We love you on TV—you're better than Elvis Presley."

On November 9, 1960, Kennedy woke up to hear that he had been voted in as the next president of the United States. It had certainly not been a landslide victory, though. In fact, it was the closest American election of the 20th century.

The Candidate

" [The film] opened with a cut of a PT boat spraying a white wake through the black night, and Kennedy was a war hero; the film next showed the quiet young man holding a book in his hand in his own library, receiving the Pulitzer Prize, and he was a scholar; then the young man held his golden-curled daughter of two, reading to her as she sat on his lap, and he was the young father; and always, gravely, open-eyed, with a sincerity that could not be feigned, he would explain his devotion to the freedom of America's faith. . . . "

Description of a documentary made for Kennedy's presidential election campaign, from The Making of the President, 1960, *by Theodore H. White.*

11

The Inauguration Speech

" Let the word go forth from this time and place, to friend and foe alike, that the torch has been passed to a new generation of Americans born in this century, tempered by war, disciplined by a hard and bitter peace, proud of our ancient heritage, and unwilling to witness or permit the slow undoing of those human rights to which this nation has always been committed, and to which we are committed today at home and around the world. "

From JFK's inauguration speech, shown above, January 20, 1961.

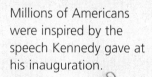

Millions of Americans were inspired by the speech Kennedy gave at his inauguration.

K ENNEDY STIRRED THE AMERICAN people. Here was a president who made them feel proud to be American, who gave them confidence, who could carry them along on the wave of optimism that was gathering momentum in the early 1960s. Kennedy's inauguration was one of the biggest celebrations in Washington for years. In his speech Kennedy's simple words appealed to everyone: "Ask not what your country can do for you, but what you can do for your country." He was asking Americans to change with the times, and under Kennedy they believed that they could. People had not yet lived through the Vietnam War or the Watergate scandal. They had faith in their politicians. It was an exciting time when people believed they could make a difference—in many ways it was the last age of innocence.

As soon as he was in office, Kennedy selected a dynamic Cabinet from what he called "the brightest and the best." It was the youngest Cabinet of the century, with an average age of just 47 years. Kennedy made bold appointments such as Robert McNamara, the politically inexperienced head of the Ford Motor Company, whom he chose as his Defense Secretary. At the risk of being seen to favor his family, he appointed his younger brother, Robert, as Attorney General. Robert Kennedy was at least someone the president could rely on. Less trustworthy was the man the president reappointed as head of the FBI (Federal Bureau of Investigation). J. Edgar Hoover was a controversial character who compiled files of information on everyone of any importance.

Hoover secretly gathered compromising information on both the Kennedy brothers, and some people even suggest he was involved in the president's assassination.

Meanwhile, the new First Lady was transforming her home. Much of the style and elegance of today's White House can be attributed to Jackie Kennedy, who restored the house to its former grandeur. Frumpy modern furniture was replaced with antiques befitting the graceful 18th-century rooms. Jackie also set up a nursery for Caroline and little John, Jr. The presence of children in the White House was a powerful vote-getter, and in 1962 Jackie hosted a televised tour of her home. Jackie also brought culture to the White House, in the form of literary dinners and music events. Jackie would call this new "kingdom" Camelot, after the legendary court of King Arthur.

TIME
THE WEEKLY NEWSMAGAZINE

SENATOR
JOHN KENNEDY.

Senator John F. Kennedy's portrait graced the cover of *Time* magazine before his election.

Kennedy claps while his daughter, Caroline, and his son, John, Jr., play in the Oval Office at the White House.

DESPITE KENNEDY'S POPULARITY, THE new president did have opposition. He was the first Catholic president, and had faced resistance from many Protestant voters. Some people also questioned whether the real man could live up to the much-hyped image. In his presidential campaigns, Kennedy had talked of a "New Frontier." Now he had to put in place the economic policies and social programs to bring it about.

In the short time (about 1,000 days) that Kennedy was in office, he set in motion many programs he himself would never see through. One of the New Frontier's major goals was to put an end to poverty. An increase in the minimum wage was passed in 1961, but plans for medical care for the elderly were defeated, as were tax cuts. Kennedy is also famous for developing the space program—in 1961 he announced his determination to send an American to the moon by the end of the decade.

One of Kennedy's most successful ideas was the founding of a volunteer organization, the Peace Corps. Under its banner, 5,000 young Americans were trained and sent to help in developing countries in Asia and Africa. By the 1990s Peace Corps volunteers were working in nearly 100 countries, but at the time critics referred to it as "Kennedy's Kiddie Korps."

When Kennedy came to power, the civil rights movement was already gaining strength. The Montgomery Bus Boycott of 1955–1956 had launched the black leader Martin Luther King, Jr. onto the civil rights stage. In Montgomery, the state capital of Alabama, a middle-aged black woman named Rosa Parks had been arrested for refusing to give up her seat on a bus to a white man.

In 1961, Kennedy awarded astronaut Alan Shepard the NASA Distinguished Service Medal for making the United States's first manned space flight.

In May 1963, peaceful black protesters in Birmingham, Alabama, were assaulted with firehoses by the army and the police.

King led a boycott of the buses, to protest against such segregation laws. After a year of protest the U.S. Supreme Court ruled bus segregation illegal. On December 21, 1956, Rosa Parks and Martin Luther King took their first ride on an integrated bus, and sat in the former "whites only" section.

In the following years, the civil rights movement staged peaceful demonstrations to protest against segregated restaurants and schools. Under the Kennedy administration, the Committee on Equal Employment Opportunity was set up. In 1962 troops were sent to the Universities of Mississippi and Alabama to force the integration of black and white students. These were positive steps but they did not defuse an increasingly volatile situation. The public was appalled when, in 1963, civil rights demonstrators in Birmingham, Alabama, were sprayed with firehoses and attacked by police dogs. In June of that year, Kennedy responded by submitting a Civil Rights Bill.

Martin Luther King, Jr. (1929–1968)

Born in Atlanta, Georgia, Martin Luther King was the founder of the Southern Christian Leadership Conference, which organized civil rights activities throughout the United States. In 1963 he led a famous civil rights march through Washington. King was initially disappointed in Kennedy, but the president gradually came to realize that social change was necessary. King helped to secure the Civil Rights Act of 1964, and was awarded the Nobel Peace Prize and the Kennedy Peace Prize. He was assassinated in Memphis, Tennessee, in 1968.

The closest threat was the communist regime of Fidel Castro in Cuba, an island in the West Indies. In 1960 President Eisenhower had broken off diplomatic relations with Cuba. Eisenhower had also planned to assassinate Castro and sponsor an invasion by anti-Castro Cubans at the Bay of Pigs on the south coast of the island. Kennedy inherited this controversial strategy, which at the time had many supporters among American military leaders. Little did Kennedy know that his approval of the operation would be considered the greatest mistake of his political career.

The Bay of Pigs invasion in April 1961 was a disaster from start to finish. Mafia men hired by the CIA (Central Intelligence Agency) to poison Castro could not get near him. An attempt to bomb Cuban air bases was mishandled. Finally, the landing at the Bay of Pigs was a failure. Castro ordered an air attack and the invasion was crushed. Meanwhile Kennedy admitted that the operation had been a terrible mistake and held back his own planned air strikes. Cuban planes then sank two American ships that lay unprotected off the coast of Cuba.

"I have to show him that we can be just as tough as he is," said President Kennedy before meeting Soviet president, Nikita Khrushchev, for the first time in June 1961.

K ENNEDY DELIGHTED IN THE way his administration was taking shape. He boasted that the smooth running of the White House switchboard meant he could be in touch with any part of the world with minimum instructions to his staff. This was important because foreign crises dominated his presidency. Most of them stemmed from the disintegrating relationship between the United States and the Soviet Union, the champions of democracy and communism, respectively. The conflict between these two "superpowers" was known as the Cold War. In the United States, "communism" became a dirty word as many Americans feared that the Soviet ideology would spread to their country. Many people had voted for Kennedy because they believed he was the man to oppose global communism. The president responded to the communist threat by building up the United States's nuclear defenses.

Fidel Castro (1927–)

The revolutionary leader Fidel Castro had ousted Cuba's corrupt president Fulgencio Batista in 1958. Upon becoming prime minister in February 1959, Castro set about reforming agriculture, industry, and education. As a poor country, Cuba struggled to get on its feet, and appealed to the United States for help. When this was refused, Cuba turned to the Soviet Union. Castro had not been a communist, but with Soviet aid Cuba quickly adopted a communist approach. The United States now had a communist nation on its doorstep.

Fidel Castro and Nikita Khrushchev join forces against the U.S.: "Why not throw a hedgehog at Uncle Sam's pants?" suggested Khrushchev, before placing missiles in Cuba.

Castro on the Bay of Pigs

" United States leaders should think that if they assist in terrorist plans to eliminate Cuban leaders, they themselves will not be safe. "

Fidel Castro, interviewed soon after the Bay of Pigs invasion.

The Bay of Pigs disaster was a massive blow to the Kennedy administration. Nearly 150 lives were lost. The CIA was angry with the president for halting air cover—if he had not changed course then, perhaps the operation would have succeeded. Kennedy lost face with his public—his first attempt at handling foreign affairs had proved an embarrassment. He was also plagued by guilt at the deaths of so many people. Fortunately for Kennedy, the opportunity to re-establish himself on the world stage was just around the corner.

MISSILE TRANSPORTERS

HEAVY EQUIPMENT

12 PROB GUIDELINE MISSILES

5 MISSILE DOLLIES

20' LONG CYLINDRICAL TANKS

MISSILE TRANSPORTERS

OPEN STORAGE

On October 14, 1962, American U-2 reconnaissance planes took aerial photographs pinpointing missile sites on Cuba.

MENTION OF THE CUBAN missile crisis of 1962 still has the power to chill anyone who lived through it—it was by far the most nerve-racking time in the history of the Cold War. For thirteen days in October, tension between the United States and the Soviet Union threatened to erupt into the horror of a full-scale nuclear war.

In April 1962, the United States had installed nuclear missiles in Turkey as a deterrent to the Soviets. In response Soviet premier Nikita Khrushchev decided to deploy nuclear missiles and thousands of troops in Cuba, which is located less than 93 miles (150 km) from Florida. If successful, this deployment would have

meant enemy nuclear missiles were within striking distance of nearly all military bases on the American mainland.

In September the Soviet government stated that all weapons sent to Cuba were for defensive purposes only. On October 15, an American spy plane photographed and identified Soviet missile-launching sites under construction in Cuba. Kennedy was warned that the sites would be operational within weeks.

For a week the world remained unaware of the crisis. It was crucial that Kennedy take a hard-line position, and he secretly urge the Soviets to halt the buildup on

Cuba. In the face of continued deployment, Kennedy had to consider appropriate action. An air strike on Cuba was deemed too dangerous to civilians, and the destruction of all missile sites could not be guaranteed. Instead Kennedy resolved to stage a naval blockade against Soviet vessels traveling to Cuba. On October 22, in a televised speech, Kennedy told the world about the situation.

Days later, Khrushchev called the American blockade "an act of aggression." The world waited for the American president's response. Kennedy stood his ground and again appealed to the Soviets to withdraw their missiles. A Soviet oil tanker was allowed through the blockade, but American intelligence reported that missile sites were still under construction. Kennedy now planned for massive air strikes. On October 26, Fidel Castro urged Khrushchev to use nuclear force against the United States if they invaded Cuba. The situation was becoming deadly.

Attorney General Robert Kennedy's negotiations with Soviet ambassador Anatoly Dobrynin, however, were making progress. On October 27, a secret agreement with the Soviets was made—the Soviet Union would remove missiles from Cuba in return for American

Fidel Castro was displeased with Khrushchev for abandoning the deployment of nuclear weapons in Cuba.

affirmation that there would be no invasion of Cuba and that missiles would be removed from Turkey.

Throughout this tense and frightening time, Kennedy remained steadfast. It was a quality that raised his status from man to myth.

Kennedy on Freedom

" The path we have chosen for the present is full of hazards, as all paths are—but it is the one most consistent with our character and courage as a nation and our commitments around the world. The cost of freedom is always high—but Americans have always paid it. And one path we shall never choose…is the path of surrender or submission. "

From Kennedy's seventeen-minute speech to the world, October 22, 1963.

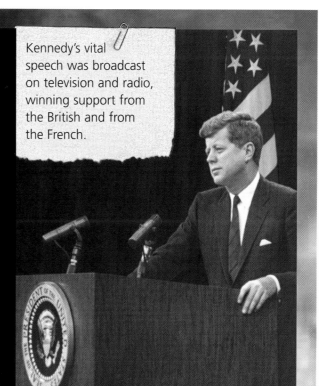

Kennedy's vital speech was broadcast on television and radio, winning support from the British and from the French.

IN 1961 THE COLD War offered Kennedy an opportunity to show his strength in Europe. After World War II Germany had been divided in two. West Germany had remained democratic, while East Germany became part of the communist Eastern Bloc. The city of Berlin, which lay deep inside East Germany, had been divided into two halves. West Berlin remained a state of West Germany, and so became a distant outpost of democracy in the heart of a communist country.

By 1961, 1,000 East Germans a day were crossing into West Berlin to secure their freedom. In response Khrushchev ordered the building of a wall of concrete and barbed wire around the border of West Berlin—the Berlin Wall. People who wished to cross the border now did so at the risk of their lives, and dozens were shot. The Wall became the most powerful symbol of communist oppression. Kennedy reinforced the American troops stationed in West Berlin. It was another show of his resolve.

In 1963 Kennedy toured Europe. He visited West Berlin, where he delivered a famous speech on freedom. It ended: "*Ich bin ein Berliner* (I am a Berliner)." Kennedy was indicating that while the immediate threat to democracy was felt in Berlin, the communist threat was felt throughout the world. By identifying free men like himself as citizens of Berlin, he united all westerners in their quest for freedom. He became a hero in Europe, too.

At home Kennedy's lifestyle appeared idyllic. The Kennedys spent weekends at luxury homes, and the beautiful First Lady was a style icon. But behind the façade of "Camelot," the Kennedy's marriage was not happy. It was rumored that the president enjoyed affairs with dozens of women—from White House secretaries to film stars such as Marilyn Monroe and Jayne Mansfield. These days such behavior might bring down a president, but the press at that time was more restrained. Kennedy remained almost unscathed.

On Kennedy's visit to West Berlin in June 1963, 150,000 people gathered to hear his speech.

The Kennedys smile for the camera, but in private the president would rant and rave about Jackie's extravagance.

By 1963 Kennedy was set for reelection the following year. But in Texas his rating was slipping. Knowing that a personal appearance was the best way of drumming up support, he planned a visit to the state for November 1963. Despite their differences, Jackie was at the president's side. On November 21, they visited San Antonio and Houston.

The following day, they were scheduled to visit Dallas.

"I can now retire from politics after having had, ah, *Happy Birthday* sung to me in such a sweet, wholesome way," Kennedy joked after Monroe's performance.

Marilyn Monroe (1926–1962)

In 1962, on the president's 45th birthday, legendary actress Marilyn Monroe sang to him before a captivated audience at Madison Square Garden. Gazing up at Kennedy, she pouted her way through *Happy Birthday, Mr. President*. But as rumors of an affair grew, Kennedy put an end to their relationship. Marilyn was heartbroken and threatened to speak to the press. A few months later, she was dead—apparently the victim of an overdose. To this day there is speculation about her death. Was it suicide, an accident, or murder?

President and Mrs. Kennedy smile at the crowds on the motorcade route. In the limousine in front of them are Texas governor John Connally, his wife, Nellie, and two Secret Service agents.

"Mr. President, you're going into a hornet's nest."
—Louisiana Congressman Hale Boggs,
November 20, 1963

THE KENNEDYS' ARRIVAL AT Love Field airbase went well, but fears for the president's safety had not quite disappeared. Kennedy was aware that he had enemies. Following a breach of security in Miami a few days earlier, his motorcade had been canceled, and Kennedy had even talked about the possibility of an assassination. Crouching down as if to avoid a bullet, he had said, "Last night would have been a hell of a night to assassinate a president."

On the morning of November 22, Kennedy had seen an advertisement placed by "The American Fact-Finding Committee" in the *Dallas Morning News*. At first the advertisement appeared genuine: "Welcome, Mr. Kennedy, to Dallas," was emblazoned across the top of the page. But underneath was a list of grievances posed as questions. Why, it asked, was he too soft on communists? The advertisement went on to cast doubt on his foreign policies, and ended on an aggressive note: "We DEMAND answers to these questions, and we want them NOW." It was an unsettling welcome to the city, causing Kennedy to comment to his wife, "Oh God, we're really heading into nut country today."

The presidential motorcade began its slow procession through the city of Dallas. John and Jackie Kennedy sat in the back of the open-topped presidential limousine, while the governor of Texas, John Connally, and his wife, Nellie, sat in the front. Moving at just 10 miles (17 km) per hour, the car edged its way through the crowded streets. The president had a 12:30 P.M. appointment for lunch, followed by a speech at the Dallas Trade Mart.

One of the last close-up photographs of the president.

A Moment in Time

As the Kennedys' limousine turns slowly down Elm Street, a man in the crowd opens an umbrella. It is the only umbrella in the crowd today, and it seems strange to see it when the sun is so hot and the crowd is so thick. Even stranger, as the president's car passes: Why does the man suddenly raise his umbrella high above his head?

Was the "umbrella man" signaling to a gunman watching from a window in the School Book Depository? The many photographs of the day show that he only kept his umbrella up while the president was on Elm Street. Before and after the assassination, the umbrella was closed. If he was signaling, this suggests that whoever killed the president did not act alone.

12:27 P.M. The motorcade traveled down Houston Street, then turned left into Elm Street and Dealey Plaza. The Plaza was a small urban park, roughly rectangular in shape. To the front and right of Elm Street, as the motorcade proceeded, was a green area that has become known as "The Grassy Knoll." At the beginning of Dealey Plaza, on the corner of Elm Street and Houston Street, was the last tall building in this part of the city—the Texas School Book Depository. This building was considered the final danger zone that the motorcade had to pass on the way to lunch, since the windows on its upper floors might offer an ideal spot for snipers.

This map of Dealey Plaza shows the route of the presidential motorcade as it passed the Texas School Book Depository and approached "The Grassy Knoll."

Texas School Book Depository

"The Grassy Knoll"

Houston Street

Main Street

Elm Street

Main Street

parking lot

Kennedy falls sideways and Jackie leans over to see what has happened. In the front of the car, Governor Connally also appears hurt.

12:29 P.M. The motorcade continued slowly along Elm Street as the Dallas sun beat mercilessly down upon an excitable and happy crowd. Throngs of people cheering and waving flags greeted the president and his smiling wife. Dallas was showing its admiration for Kennedy's courage in coming into hostile territory. The presence of fanatical groups in the South had caused alarm, but fears for the president's safety were beginning to fade. Nellie Connally turned and smiled at the president, and said, "Mr. Kennedy, you can't say Dallas doesn't love you." "That is very obvious," he replied.

12:31 P.M. Suddenly, a loud cracking noise sent a shudder through everyone. There was no time to piece together the unbelievable spectacle taking place. Comprehending the cold-blooded murder of a president takes longer than the

couple of seconds it takes to gun him down. The president was clasping his throat. His wife and Governor Connally turned to him with puzzled expressions. There was another cracking sound, which was now recognizable as gunfire, and a blur of red. The president was thrown violently back against his leather seat. Governor Connally slumped back in his own seat, also hit.

The car slowed down. Jackie Kennedy was screaming. She began clambering out onto the back of the limousine, as if trying to escape this terrible nightmare. Secret Service agent Clint Hill dashed up and pulled Jackie back inside. Then the limousine began picking up speed. The driver turned toward Parkland Hospital. Nellie Connally later reported Jackie's stunned response: "I love you, Jack...Jack...they've killed my husband...I have his brains in my hands."

Secret Service agent Clint Hill pulls Jackie back into the limousine as it begins to speed away from the scene.

12:35 P.M. When the limousine pulled up at the hospital, Jackie was leaning protectively over the body of her husband. In truth, she did not want anyone to see his horrific wounds—the whole right side of his head had been blown away. Blood was spattered over the interior of the car and Jackie's pink Chanel suit. Governor Connally was unconscious next to his weeping wife.

The president's life was seeping away as the bloodstain down the side of his gray suit grew ominously.

A Moment in Time

Abraham Zapruder is in the crowd on this day, clasping a movie camera. He has a good view of the motorcade and starts filming as the president and his wife smile and wave to the cheering crowds on Elm Street. The next eighteen seconds of film capture the full horror of events, as Zapruder finds himself filming a terrible moment in history—the assassination of a president.

The amateur footage known as the Zapruder Film *became vital to investigations into Kennedy's death. Its blurry color images are rarely shown, and were not televised until 1975. Viewing the film gives a strange reality to an historical moment that is still difficult to comprehend.*

Spectators lie on the grass to avoid further gunfire, as photographers and news cameramen continue filming.

12:40 P.M. Miraculously, when President Kennedy was rushed into Parkland Hospital, he still had a pulse. The trauma team went through their drill but knew it was hopeless from the start. They determined that the president had been shot in the neck and in the head.

1:00 P.M. Doctors pronounced President John F. Kennedy dead. Outside the hospital crowds awaited news of their president; few realized that Kennedy had been mortally injured when he was shot in Dealey Plaza. After two priests entered the hospital just before 1:00 P.M., people began to lose hope. When one of the priests left the hospital, he confirmed that he had just performed the last rites on the president. People were numb with shock.

1:33 P.M. The White House confirmed the tragic news: John F. Kennedy was dead. People everywhere wept openly. From this point everything happened very quickly. Lyndon B. Johnson, the vice president, was present at Parkland Hospital. He was determined to get the president's body back to Washington as soon as possible. Johnson, who would automatically become the next president of the United States, also had his own security at stake. At this point, there was a real fear that the Soviet Union might take advantage of the hysteria and bomb the United States.

On board Air Force One, Lyndon B. Johnson takes the oath of office, with a shocked Jackie Kennedy by his side.

2:20 P.M. By this time Kennedy's body had been transported to Love Field airbase, accompanied by a group including Johnson and Jackie Kennedy. Security had been stepped up, and there is no footage of Kennedy's coffin being transferred to Air Force One—the plane that would transport the president's body back to Washington.

2:38 P.M. On board Air Force One, Lyndon B. Johnson was sworn in as the new president, with Jackie Kennedy at his side. After the formal oath had been taken, Jackie sat down next to her husband's coffin. Less than three hours before, she had been with the president as he campaigned for the next election.

Now she sat in stunned silence, still wearing the blood-stained pink suit that she refused to take off. "Let them see what they've done," she said.

5:59 P.M. It was getting dark when Air Force One landed at Andrews Air Force Base in Washington. Robert Kennedy boarded the plane immediately. Later he accompanied Jackie out of the plane. Holding hands, they appeared bound together in grief. For the first time, the world saw the ex-First Lady—it was shocking to see her smeared in blood and battling for composure. And her day was not over yet—she wanted to travel with her husband's body to Bethesda Naval Hospital, where an autopsy would be performed overnight.

Security guards carry Kennedy's coffin from the plane. Robert Kennedy did not leave Jackie's side for the rest of the weekend.

A Moment in Time

On the night of the assassination, the president's body arrives at Bethesda Naval Hospital. But the autopsy carried out there does not seem to follow normal procedures. The president's head is never shaved, so it is impossible for pathologists to determine the exact injuries and the entry and exit wounds made by the bullets. Photographs of the president's brain are taken, along with X rays and blood samples. These are sent to the president's former secretary, but they mysteriously disappear.

Were the botched autopsy and missing results caused by panic? Or was somebody trying to hide something?

The controversial photograph used in the case against Oswald. Supposedly taken in 1963, Oswald is holding up the rifle said to have been used in the shooting of Kennedy. Some people claim the picture is a fake.

12:32 P.M. We can only imagine the confusion and chaos on the crowded streets of Dallas in the aftermath of the shooting. But it did not take long for the police to single out Oswald. Hardly a minute after the shots that killed the president had been fired, a police officer spotted Oswald in the canteen at the Texas School Book Depository. Officers had quickly entered the building, believing shots had come from the sixth floor. The police officer who saw Oswald noted his relaxed appearance.

A Moment in Time

On the morning of November 22, Lee Harvey Oswald enters the Texas Book Depository where he works. Colleagues see him carrying a long object in a brown paper bag. According to Oswald's later testimony, this is not a rifle but a bundle of curtain rods. At 12:31 P.M., shots are fired from the sixth floor of the Book Depository. Oswald certainly seems to have been here at some point, because his fingerprints are later found on cardboard boxes.

About ninety minutes later, Oswald is arrested. He is carrying false ID in the name of A. Hidell. A rifle found on the sixth floor of the Book Depository is traced to this name. Back at Oswald's lodgings, police officers find photographs of him holding the rifle. Oswald is later picked out at a lineup as a man at the scene of police officer J. D. Tippit's murder. Did Oswald kill Tippit and Kennedy? Or was he framed as a "patsy," or scapegoat, as he always claimed to the police?

WHILE EVERYBODY WAS ASKING *why* somebody would kill the president, there was little time to consider *who* had killed him—the Dallas police quickly claimed they had their man. Lee Harvey Oswald was arrested within ninety minutes of the shooting, and was charged with John F. Kennedy's murder at 1:30 A.M. on the morning of November 23, 1963.

Another photograph that pinned the blame on Oswald, showing him in 1963 distributing "Hands off Cuba" leaflets in New Orleans, Louisiana.

Inset: Oswald with his wife, Marina, and their baby.

12:40 P.M. Oswald was spotted again just eight minutes later, this time boarding a bus away from Dealey Plaza. He then took another bus back to Dealey Plaza. At 12:54 P.M. he was seen getting out of a cab a few blocks from his boarding house. At 1:00 P.M. Oswald grabbed a jacket and a pistol from his lodgings, before heading for a bus stop. Oswald's movements that day were certainly suspicious. But if he was indeed the assassin and was trying to escape, why did he take the second bus back to Dealey Plaza?

1:15 P.M. Dallas police officer J. D. Tippit was shot dead in the street. At 1:40 P.M., six streets from the scene of Tippit's murder, a shop manager noticed a man duck into his shop as a police car drove past. He watched him head into a movie theater and called the police. At about 1:50 P.M. police rushed into the theater—and arrested Lee Harvey Oswald.

He was in possession of a .38 caliber revolver that contained all of its bullets. It was never proved that cartridges found at the scene of Tippit's murder were from Oswald's gun. Oswald was charged with Tippit's murder. Later that night, he was charged with killing the president.

The police needed to make a quick arrest to curb public hysteria—and as a suspect, Lee Harvey Oswald was almost too good to be true. He was an ex-Marine who had lived in the Soviet Union and was married to a Soviet woman, Marina Prusakova. He was a communist supporter, and had moved to Dallas in November 1962. In August 1963, he had been arrested for distributing leaflets supporting Cuba, and a month before the assassination he had attempted to obtain a visa to enter that country.

Oswald had both the motive and the means—in March 1963, he had purchased a high-powered rifle.

AMERICANS WERE DEVASTATED BY the death of their president. Eyewitness reports from Dallas filled the newspapers, television documentaries about the president dominated the airwaves, and people everywhere expressed their grief. On Saturday, November 23, it was announced that Oswald, who was still being held in the city jail at Dallas police headquarters, would be transferred the next morning to the county jail on Houston Street in Dealey Plaza.

On Sunday morning, November 24, live television once again brought history into people's living rooms. Twenty million viewers watched as Oswald was escorted by two policemen from the building. Police officers and about 75 reporters crowded around the entrance. Somebody shouted, "Do you have anything to say in your defense?" Oswald had no time to reply. A man pushed through the crowds and shot him in the stomach at point-blank range. Oswald doubled up in agony. There was a scuffle as the gunman was overpowered and led away. Oswald was rushed to Parkland Hospital, where he died that afternoon.

With Oswald dead, there would be no trial to determine the president's killer. There would be no opportunity for the main suspect to defend himself.

A Moment in Time

At 1:25 P.M. on November 24, Lee Harvey Oswald is pronounced dead. The man he was accused of assassinating had died in the very same hospital almost exactly 48 hours earlier. The press gathers to hear the facts in the same room in which they had gathered to hear news of their president. Just as Oswald is pronounced dead, a memorial ceremony for John F. Kennedy at the Capitol building in Washington comes to an end.

Jack Ruby bursts through the crowd and shoots Oswald in the stomach. How was Ruby allowed to slip past policemen and target Oswald at such close range?

Lee Harvey Oswald's murderer was Jack Ruby, a nightclub owner. His execution of Oswald appealed to some people's sense of justice, but it also led to sinister theories. Was Oswald being silenced by a powerful group that had masterminded the president's killing? It was suggested that Ruby had Mafia connections, but as with most theories about John F. Kennedy's death, nothing is certain. Ruby was convicted of Oswald's murder, but was staging an appeal when he died of lung cancer in 1967.

An official body called the Warren Commission was created to investigate the assassination. A panel of distinguished citizens was selected to comb through every aspect of the murder. Headed by Chief Justice Earl Warren, the commission was granted help from all the American federal agencies, including the FBI and the CIA. It would be nine months before the commission published its report, and in the meantime Americans speculated and mourned.

The Claims of Jack Ruby

"No underworld person made any effort to contact me. It all happened that Sunday morning....The last thing I read was that Mrs. Kennedy may have to come back to Dallas for a trial for Lee Harvey Oswald...someone owed this debt to our beloved president to save her the ordeal of coming back. I had the gun in my right hip pocket, and impulsively, if that is the correct word here, I saw him and that is all I can say...I think I used the words, 'You killed my president, you rat.'"

Jack Ruby, seven months after the assassination, Dallas County Jail.

Jack Ruby
(top right) photographed at a press conference held by Dallas police on the evening of Kennedy's assassination. Was he stalking Oswald?

ONDAY, NOVEMBER 25, 1963, was a solemn occasion. John F. Kennedy was buried, and there was an official day of mourning. A hush fell on the streets of the United States as schools, shops, and businesses shut down. Churches everywhere held special services. In Washington the previous day and night, 250,000 people had filed past the late president's flag-draped coffin as it lay in state at the Capitol building.

At 11:30 A.M. a procession formed outside the White House. It was a somber gathering that included world leaders Prince Philip of Britain, President Charles de Gaulle of France, and Emperor Haile Selassie of Ethiopia. Jackie Kennedy insisted upon walking beside the carriage that carried Kennedy's coffin to St. Matthew's Cathedral for the requiem mass. Robert Kennedy and other members of the Kennedy family remained at her side. Church bells tolled throughout the city, and bagpipes accompanied the slow march.

Following the service, Kennedy's coffin was taken to Arlington National Cemetery. One million mourners lined the route to the cemetery. On the steps of the cathedral, little John Kennedy, Jr. stood up straight and saluted his father. This powerful image, which was printed in newspapers around the world, touched a nerve. Joined together in their sorrow, people wept and hugged each other. Television cameras transmitted the sad scenes throughout a world that was united in grief.

At the cemetery the *Star-Spangled Banner* was played by a military band, fifty planes performed a fly by and soldiers fired a 21-gun salute. After the service Jackie lit an eternal flame at the graveside of her

On the steps of St. Matthew's Cathedral, Jackie Kennedy holds the hands of her young children. Before them is the flag-draped coffin of John F. Kennedy.

husband, which would burn forever in his memory. Finally, John F. Kennedy was laid to rest.

The drama that had been played out over the previous four days had ended. Jackie Kennedy, whose dignity throughout the proceedings touched people's hearts, had said goodbye to her husband in the way she wanted. But at 6:00 P.M. in the White House, there was another "ceremony." The day of John F. Kennedy's funeral was also the day of John Kennedy, Jr.'s third birthday. Jackie now had to host a party for her son.

This enduring image of three-year-old John, Jr. as he salutes his father's coffin was used in newspapers and magazines around the world—it still evokes the emotion of the occasion.

A Moment in Time

Three funerals are held on November 25, 1963. In Washington, D.C., the world watches as John F. Kennedy is buried with military honors. In Dallas 700 police officers attend the funeral of Officer J. D. Tippit. The man accused of murdering them both, Lee Harvey Oswald, is also buried on this day. Only his mother, brother, wife, and children attend the service, and reporters have to act as pallbearers.

THE DRAMA OF THE Kennedy assassination has never really ended. The unsatisfactory report published by the Warren Commission in September 1964 kept the controversy alive. The Commission concluded that only three shots were fired that day, all by Lee Harvey Oswald from the sixth floor of the Texas School Book Depository. They claimed that one bullet struck a bystander in the crowd, while two bullets hit the president.

To support its claim that only three shots had been fired, the Commission put forward what has been called the "magic bullet" theory. They stated that a single bullet had entered the president's throat, exited, entered Governor Connally's back, exited his chest, entered and broken his wrist, and finally buried itself in his leg. The Commission relied on this "magic bullet" to dismiss claims that some injuries had been caused by shots from a second gunman. In summary the Commission claimed that Oswald had acted alone and without the support of a major organization (such as the Mafia) or a foreign power (such as Cuba). In other words, there had been no conspiracy.

The Warren Commission had been set up as an independent body, but was backed by the CIA and the FBI. J. Edgar Hoover, the head of the FBI, was happy with the Commission's simple solution—he did not want people investigating the files he kept on the Kennedys. The CIA was also nervous about conspiracy theories. It had hired the Mafia to kill Castro during the Bay of Pigs fiasco, so any Mafia involvement in the Kennedy assassination would implicate the CIA. If the assassination was shown to be a revenge attack by the Cubans, the CIA would again be accountable. Because of these assumptions, the Warren Commission decision has been questioned.

However, it is the eyewitness accounts of November 22, 1963, that really cloud the issue. Many people claimed they heard gunfire coming from "The Grassy Knoll" in Dealey Plaza (see map on page 23), and others say they saw smoke there. There were also numerous sightings of men with rifles in the crowd that day.

Members of the Warren Commission gather during the investigation in 1964, led by Supreme Court Chief Justice Earl Warren (center, in glasses).

The Warren Commission reenacted the assassination. Here, on the sixth floor of the Texas School Book Depository, an expert tries to determine the trajectories of the bullets fired at Kennedy.

Inset: The view of the president's limousine from the sixth floor of the Book Depository, as set up by the Warren Commission.

Connally's Testimony

" ...The thought immediately passed through my mind that there were two or three people involved, or more, in this; or that someone was shooting with an automatic rifle. "

Governor John Connally recalling the moment of the assassination, in which he was injured.

The Warren Commission's three-bullet theory relied upon the fatal bullet hitting the president from behind. Without the missing autopsy report it was impossible to prove or disprove this. But the Zapruder Film, which the Commission used to determine how many bullets had been fired, shows the president's head being blown backward as though shot from the front. A gunman positioned on "The Grassy Knoll" would have fired from the front, but it would have been impossible to shoot at this angle from the sixth floor of the Texas School Book Depository.

Had the Warren Commission made a full and accurate report of the day's events?

Jack Ruby speaking to journalists in February 1964. If there had been a conspiracy to kill Kennedy and silence his assassin, Ruby certainly was not saying.

WE MAY NEVER KNOW the truth about Kennedy's death. There are many different conspiracy theories, suggesting that the CIA, the FBI, anti-Castro Cubans, Fidel Castro, or the Mafia had planned the assassination. More difficult to believe are suggestions that presidents Lyndon B. Johnson or Richard Nixon had some involvement in Kennedy's death. Some of the theories have little evidence to support them, and most have been proven untrue. Still, some people remain unconvinced by the Warren Report's conclusion that Oswald acted alone.

The Mafia

This theory originated in whispers of Jack Ruby's connections to the Mafia. Kennedy's father, Joe, had Mafia connections too, and he used them on his son's behalf during the 1960 elections. Sam Giancana, head of the Chicago Mafia, helped Kennedy to win votes in Cook County, Chicago, which were vital to Kennedy's victory in the election. The Kennedy administration later tried to curb organized crime, and Kennedy broke off contact with Sam Giancana. Not long before Kennedy's death, Mafia chiefs were overheard plotting to kill the president.

Fidel Castro

Fidel Castro denied any involvement in the assassination, but having survived an assassination attempt on his own life by the Kennedy administration, he had every motive. When the CIA hired the Mafia to kill Castro, the mobster in charge was Sam Giancana's number two, Johnny Roselli. He later claimed that Castro ordered the assassination. So did President Lyndon B. Johnson, who off the record said, "Castro got to Kennedy before Kennedy got to Castro."

Different Views

" While the question, 'Who killed President Kennedy?' is important, the question, 'What killed him?' is more important. Our late president was assassinated by a morally inclement climate ....It is a climate where men cannot disagree without being disagreeable, and they express dissent through violence and murder. "

Martin Luther King, Jr., in 1963. King was himself assassinated in 1968.

" Being an old farm boy myself, chickens coming home to roost never did make me sad; they've always made me glad...the seeds that America had sown—in enslavement, in many things that followed since then—all these seeds were coming up today; it was harvest time. "

Malcolm X, black civil rights campaigner and extremist, on the assassination of Kennedy.

Anti-Castro Cubans

There was another group of Cubans who had a motive to kill Kennedy. Anti-Castro Cubans who had anticipated success at the Bay of Pigs were furious with Kennedy for withholding air cover. They blamed him for the failure of the invasion. Was the assassination their ultimate revenge?

Richard Nixon

Nixon flew into Dallas on November 20, 1963, and left on the morning of Kennedy's assassination. He later claimed that he had been to a meeting at the Pepsi-Cola Company. Records from the company show that there was no such meeting. What was Nixon doing in Dallas at this crucial time?

Supporters of Fidel Castro gather outside the Presidential Palace in Havana shortly before the Bay of Pigs fiasco in 1961. Was Kennedy's assassination the Cubans' revenge for the attack on their country?

THE PUBLIC HAD ENJOYED a very special bond with their president, and many were delighted that there was another young and vibrant Kennedy willing to pick up the political torch. Shortly after his brother's death, Robert Kennedy resigned as Attorney General, but by August 1964 he was running for a Senate seat in New York. In the same month, at the Democratic National Convention, he spoke movingly about his brother (see sidebar opposite) and showed the public that he too had the strength and commitment to lead his country.

In 1968 Robert Kennedy began his own campaign to become president of the United States. The world had changed a lot since the death of his brother. The Civil Rights Act had been passed in 1964, prohibiting racial discrimination in employment, education, unions, public accommodations, and restaurants. In 1965, the Voting Rights Act had made it illegal to impose literacy tests or poll taxes upon voters, a system that had been used mostly to keep blacks from voting in the South. But there were still ongoing race riots. Also, American troops were still fighting a war in Vietnam that had begun before JFK became president. Some now felt this war was both senseless and contrary to the spirit of freedom favored by a western democracy.

Robert Kennedy promised to be a different kind of president. John F. Kennedy had been cautious about civil rights, but Robert Kennedy championed the cause. He wanted equality for black people, and promised them more rights and a better education.

Robert Kennedy and his wife visit Coretta Scott King, the widow of Martin Luther King, Jr., following King's assassination. Kennedy would himself be assassinated a short time later.

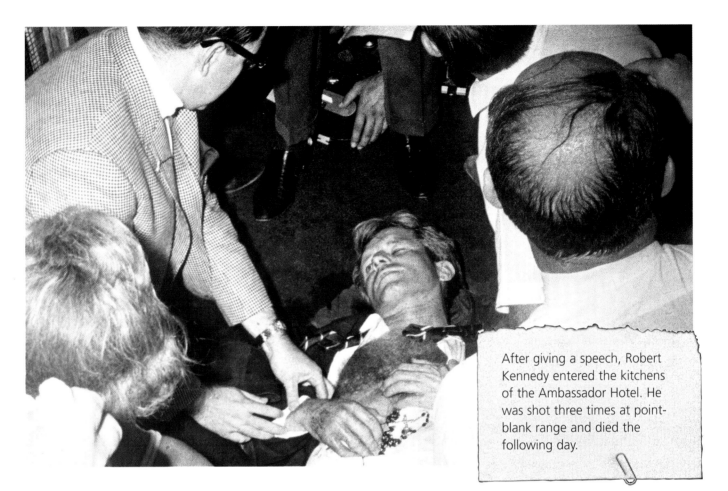

After giving a speech, Robert Kennedy entered the kitchens of the Ambassador Hotel. He was shot three times at point-blank range and died the following day.

On the question of Vietnam he was vocal, too. As President Johnson increased American intervention, Robert Kennedy spoke out against the war. Many young Americans, black and white and spanning the social scale, believed Robert Kennedy was the man for these difficult times.

Their hopes were cut short by another assassination. Robert Kennedy was gunned down on June 5, 1968, at the Ambassador Hotel in Los Angeles, by a Jordanian immigrant named Sirhan Sirhan.

Robert Kennedy's reputation had been established by his quest for civil rights and his stance against the Vietnam War. He often quoted George Bernard Shaw in his speeches: "Some men see things as they are and ask 'Why?' I dream of things that never were and ask 'Why not?'" But after the assassinations of the Kennedy brothers, the majority of Americans were left asking themselves "Why?"

Looking to the Future

"I know that it was a source of great strength to him [JFK] to know that there were thousands of people all over the United States who were together with him, dedicated to certain principles and to certain ideals....I realize that as individuals, and even more important, as a political party and as a country, we can't just look to the past, we must look to the future."

Robert Kennedy, speaking at the Democratic National Convention, August 27, 1964.

WHAT IF, ON November 22, 1963, the presidential motorcade had passed safely through Dealey Plaza? How would the United States and the world have been different, had John F. Kennedy lived?

Kennedy's death possibly accelerated the passage of some of his social reforms through Congress. Without his death, would there have been a Civil Rights Act of 1964? Kennedy had been cautious about civil rights, but in June 1963 he had submitted his Civil Rights Bill. He had organized a meeting with Martin Luther King, Jr. and other black leaders, following the civil rights march of August 28, 1963, at which King had given his famous "I have a dream" speech. These actions had made Kennedy less popular with his white voters—perhaps the Civil Rights Bill would not have had such an easy passage through Congress, if it had not been carried out in his memory.

There is also the vital question of the Vietnam War. For the last months of his presidency, Kennedy had become increasingly concerned by the United States's involvement in the war. In television interviews in September 1963, he had said that he would continue to defend South Vietnam against communism, but also insisted that it was South Vietnam's war. He stated, "They are the ones who have to win it or lose it."

Kennedy had been sickened by CIA involvement in the killing of South Vietnam's dictator president Ngo Dinh Diem in early November 1963, and wanted to distance himself from events there. In the few weeks before his own assassination, Kennedy was probably calculating how to get the United States out of the war. We cannot know this for certain, but there is evidence that once the 1964 election was over he might have tried to gradually reduce American military involvement in Vietnam.

John and Jackie Kennedy, with Vice President Lyndon B. Johnson, at a breakfast in Fort Worth, Texas, on the day of the assassination. If Kennedy had listened to advisers, he might never have flown to Dallas later that morning.

U.S. troops in Vietnam in 1968. The war lasted until 1975, and 200,000 South Vietnamese soldiers, one million North Vietnamese soldiers, 500,000 civilians, and 56,555 American soldiers were killed. Would this have happened, had Kennedy lived?

Finally, if Kennedy had not died, would Americans be the same people they are today? Some people say that optimism died with him. With the conspiracy theories surrounding Kennedy's death came the revelations about his private life. Americans discovered that the Kennedy myth was flawed. It is difficult to imagine people being so dazzled by a politician again. Ever since Kennedy's death, the media has been a willing watchdog ready to pounce when politicians step out of line. Now people question the television reports they watch and the newspaper articles they read. They have come a long way since November 22, 1963.

It is said that Kennedy tried to warn Diem about an assassination attempt, but Diem refused to heed the warning.

Moments in Time

Kennedy is not the only world leader to be assassinated in November 1963. In South Vietnam, on November 2 , a group of army generals murder their president, Ngo Dinh Diem. Kennedy is genuinely shocked. Some people say that American involvement in the plot depresses him as much as the Bay of Pigs disaster. Diem's assassination is part of a coup backed by the CIA. It is believed that the CIA may have been acting against the president's wishes.

After the Diem assassination, Kennedy may have been considering reducing the CIA's powers. Did the CIA plan Kennedy's assassination before he could do this? Did one assassination in November 1963 lead to another?

41

Less than a week before his death, Kennedy visited Cape Canaveral Space Center. When he launched the Space Program in 1961, Kennedy had hoped that an American would reach the moon by 1970. The mission was completed in July 1969.

THE UNITED STATES HAS COME to terms with the death of John F. Kennedy, and has held onto the myth that grew up around him. Despite the revelations surrounding his private life, Kennedy still tops the polls for the best American president. Of his contemporaries, Lyndon B. Johnson is remembered for continuing the Vietnam War, while Richard Nixon was exposed by the Watergate scandal.

Kennedy was killed just when his domestic and international policies seemed to be coming to fruition. He also died before he could show the world the full extent of his talents as a head of state. He was one of several 20th-century icons who were murdered while still young—men like Robert Kennedy, Martin Luther King, Jr., Malcolm X, John Lennon. With Kennedy, as with them all, we mourn not just the loss of the person, but what he might have gone on to achieve.

We can only guess how Kennedy would have handled the dark days of the late 1960s. He had bolstered the United States's nuclear deterrent and stood firm against communist expansion, thus shaping the ongoing Cold War. He had also hinted at a withdrawal that might have ended the seemingly endless war in Vietnam. Domestically Kennedy's New Frontier established the ground for Johnson's "Great Society" program of economic and social welfare reforms. Kennedy's plans for medical care for the elderly were realized in Johnson's 1965 Medicare program, and the Civil Rights Act of 1964 may be seen as part of Kennedy's legacy. In spite of this, there were race riots and student protests. Many young people joined the hippie movement, and dropped out of a fragmenting society. Perhaps these violent shifts and changes can be seen as a legacy of the act of violence that robbed the United States of its president.

Most people alive at the time can remember where they were when they heard the news of Kennedy's assassination.

Two events that had a similar impact on 20th-century history would have been unthinkable without Kennedy's influence. In 1969 Neil Armstrong's first steps on the moon fulfilled an extraordinary promise made by Kennedy at the beginning of the decade. Twenty years later, the Berlin Wall, which symbolized Cold War divisions, was torn down—a triumph for freedom and democracy that can trace its roots back to the moment Kennedy visited Berlin to defend those very principles.

Finally, the death of Kennedy has left a legacy of uncertainty. Writers continue to speculate about who was behind the assassination. In 1981 Oswald's body was even disinterred in an attempt to solve the mystery. Until this question is answered without a degree of doubt, Kennedy's story will remain unfinished.

The Kennedy Curse

The "Kennedy Curse" has claimed the lives of Joseph Kennedy, John F. Kennedy, Robert Kennedy; the political careers of Joe and Edward (Ted) Kennedy; and most recently the life of John Kennedy, Jr. In July 1999, the plane he was flying crashed into the Atlantic. The nation had watched his goodbye salute to his father as a three-year-old boy in 1963. His untimely death brought the tragic story full circle.

In the shadow of the Berlin Wall, West Berliners mourn the death of President Kennedy in November 1963.

Glossary

Attorney General The chief legal officer in some countries, including the United States.

autopsy The medical examination carried out to establish cause of death.

baby boomer A child born during a time of increasing birth rate. It usually refers to the post-World War II generation.

Cabinet A committee of politicians selected by the president to head national agencies and establish government policy.

caliber The size of a gun barrel, and therefore of the bullets it fires.

Capitol The building in Washington, D.C., where Congress meets.

CIA (Central Intelligence Agency) The federal government body responsible for collecting information of military or political value.

civil rights The rights of individuals to equality and justice, particularly those fought for by blacks and women in the United States.

communism A system in which society is classless and all property is collectively owned. This was the system used by the Soviet Union from 1917 to 1989.

Congress The U.S. Congress is composed of the Senate and the House of Representatives, and its members propose and vote on new laws.

conservative Opposed to rapid change, in favor of preserving traditional values.

Democratic Party One of the United States's two main political parties.

Democratic National Convention The annual meeting of the Democratic party for members from all states.

democracy A form of government in which people rule through their elected leaders.

depository A storehouse or warehouse.

diplomatic relations The relationship between governments of different countries.

disinterred Dug up, taken out of a grave.

façade An outward appearance that may hide what is really happening.

FBI (Federal Bureau of Investigation) The government body that deals mainly with internal security and law enforcement in the United States.

finishing school A school where some girls finish their education by learning social refinements.

First Lady The president's wife.

inauguration The ceremony admitting a new president to office.

inclement Cold, hostile, or stormy.

integrated Joined together, particularly by removing racial segregation.

last rites A religious ceremony administered to a dying person.

Mafia An organized body of criminals, usually involved in various activities such as gambling, prostitution, and drugs.

motorcade A procession of motor vehicles.

NASA National Aeronautics and Space Administration, the agency in charge of the United States's space program.

New Frontier The administration, policies, and program of President Kennedy from 1961–1963.

Nobel Peace Prize An award given each year to the person or organization that has made the greatest contribution to world peace.

pallbearers People who carry the coffin at a funeral.

pathologist   A doctor who specializes in disease and causes of death.

PT boat   A Patrol Torpedo motorboat.

Pulitzer Prize   A prize awarded in the United States for outstanding achievement in various areas, including biographical literature.

Purple Heart   The American military medal awarded to those wounded in battle.

Republican Party   One of the United States's two main political parties.

segregation   The separation of different racial groups.

Senate   The Senate is part of the U.S. Congress, and is made up of two members (senators) from each state.

status quo   The existing or normal state of affairs.

Stock Exchange   The association of dealers who organize the buying and selling of stocks and shares.

superpower   A dominant country in world politics, such as the United States or Soviet Union during the Cold War.

trajectory   The path that an object, such as a bullet, takes through space or air.

trauma team   A team of doctors and nurses that specializes in treating accidents and emergencies.

trust funds   Money or property managed by one party for the benefit of somebody else, such as their children.

United Nations (UN)   An organization established in October 1945 to work for world peace, which now has representatives from most of the world's nations.

Vietnam War   The war fought from 1957 to 1975, between communist North Vietnam and South Vietnamese forces supported by American troops.

Watergate   The scandal over illegal activities that helped Nixon to win the 1972 presidential election, and resulted in Nixon's resignation in 1974.

Further Information

Sources

Bornemann Spies, Karen. *John F. Kennedy*. Berkeley Heights, NJ: Enslow Publishers, 1999.

Coulter, Laurie. *When John and Caroline Lived in the White House*. Fayetteville, AR: Hyperion Press, 2000.

Donnelly, Judy. *Who Shot the President?* New York: Random House, 1998.

Grant, R.G. *The Berlin Wall*. New York: Raintree Steck-Vaughn Publishers, 1998.

Kent, Zachary. *John F. Kennedy, Thirty-Fifth President of the United States*. San Francisco, CA: Children's Press, 1987.

Taylor, David. *The Cold War*. Chicago, IL: Heinemann Library, 2001.

Time Line

May 27, 1917   John F. Kennedy is born in Brookline, Massachusetts.

November 20, 1925   Robert Kennedy is born in Brookline, Massachusetts.

1943   John F. Kennedy serves in the Pacific during World War II, and is decorated for his heroism.

1946   Kennedy, only 29 years old, is elected as a Democratic congressman from Massachusetts.

1952   Kennedy is elected to the Senate.

September 12, 1953   Kennedy marries Jacqueline Bouvier in Newport, Rhode Island.

1956   Kennedy writes *Profiles in Courage* which is awarded the Pulitzer Prize.

November 1957   The Kennedys' first child, Caroline Kennedy, is born.

September 26, 1960   Kennedy and Nixon appear in the first live television debate between a Republican and a Democratic presidential nominee.

November 9, 1960   Kennedy is elected president.

November 25, 1960   The Kennedys' second child, John Jr., is born.

April 15–20, 1961   The Bay of Pigs invasion of Cuba fails.

October 1961   Kennedy sends American troops into West Berlin. U.S. military advisers are sent to Vietnam to assess the situation there.

February 1962   Jackie Kennedy lets television cameras tour the White House. Some 80 million Americans see inside the restored mansion for the first time.

May 27, 1962   Marilyn Monroe sings *Happy Birthday* to the president at Madison Square Garden, on his 45th birthday.

October 15–27, 1962   The Cuban Missile Crisis shakes the world. Kennedy's diplomacy averts a nuclear war.

November 22, 1963   Kennedy is assassinated in Dallas, Texas.

June 5, 1968   Robert Kennedy is assassinated in Los Angeles.

May 19, 1994   Jackie Kennedy dies of cancer in New York.

July 17, 1999   John, Jr. and his wife and sister-in-law are killed in a plane crash.

An eternal flame burns constantly over the grave of John F. Kennedy in Arlington National Cemetery, Virginia.

Index